SPORT & ST PAUL

A COURSE

FOR CHAMPIONS

by
Edio Costantini
&
Kevin Lixey, LC

Preface by
Jack Del Rio

Originally published in Italian as:

San Paolo e lo Sport: un percorso per campioni

© 2009 Edizioni La Meridiana

Molfetta (BARI)

Translated by Daniela Pipe

(translations@pipe.org.uk)

©2011 English text, Edio Costantini & Kevin Lixey, L.C.

The John Paul II Sports Foundation, Rome

ISBN 978-1-4709-8991-0

for athletes, coaches and educators

CONTENTS

I have fought the good fight, I have finished the race, I have kept the faith. From now on there is reserved for me the crown of righteousness, which the Lord, the righteous judge, will give me on that day...

2 Tim. 4: 7-8

PREFACE

Sport, in many ways, is a microcosm of life and often serves as a training ground for the realities of daily living. During a typical season of football in the NFL, we will experience frustration, physical and mental fatigue, the joys of winning and the disappointments of losing. Yet, through it all, we must maintain our disposition, we must have patience and we must keep the faith and not become discouraged. We learn how to compete, even when we are exhausted, and we learn how much the team will benefit when we are willing to sacrifice for each other, just as Christ sacrificed for us. Team sports are fantastic avenues to teach these virtues and offer valuable life lessons.

In October 2000, Pope John Paul II held a Jubilee for Sport. Here are a few excerpts from his homily given on this occasion in Rome's Olympic Stadium. Sports "can develop important values such as loyalty, perseverance, friendship, sharing and solidarity." He continued: "Persevering effort is needed to succeed in life. Anyone who plays sport knows this very well. It is only at the cost of strenuous training that significant results are achieved for 'Those who sow in tears will reap with cries of joy' (Ps. 126: 5)."

In this way, sports also offer rich analogies for the spiritual life. In fact, almost all of Paul's letters – as you are about to see in the pages that follow– contain sports related metaphors that help to convey valuable lessons for our life of faith as well as for athletics. They mark a course for champions.

Being asked to write the preface to this book is no coincidence, for I believe God works in a purposeful manner. He has his own design for each soul. So, I know very well that I must rely on God to guide my thoughts as I prayerfully set out to make a few comments that I hope will help to inspire you as these beautifully illustrations on the sports analogies and images in St Paul have inspired me. As each of the following chapters in this book begin with words from St Paul's letters, I want to do the same, quoting from Paul's letter to the Romans: "We know that all things work for good for those who love God, who are called according to his purpose" (Rom 8:28).

This idea that all things —and that all people— can work for the overall good struck me in a special way while visiting Rome. On the last day of the year of St Paul — who is, by the way, one of my favorite saints! – while attending the Evening Prayer service presided by Pope Benedict XVI in the Basilica of St Paul Outside the Walls, my family and I were surrounded by people from all over the world. There were so many different backgrounds, life experiences and cultures…but in that moment, we were all connected. It was a great display of how God uses us all, no matter who we are or where we are from, to fulfill his purpose. We simply need to hear his call and answer it.

I pray that the Holy Spirit will help me in this undertaking and I pray that you will open your hearts and join me and countless others in this "mission". You see, we really are on a mission…a sport's mission. Our children need us, this entire generation needs us, and sports are a wonderful conduit to reach our youth and guide them to maturity. They need somebody who will carry the torch, somebody willing to stand up for what is true, what is wholesome and what is right. Too often the examples that are lifted up, celebrated or hyped are steeped in the win at all costs, cheat if you have to, be completely selfish mentalities.

This year I enter my 26th season as a member of a professional sports team: eleven of those years as a player and fifteen as a coach. While now in my 9th season as the head coach for the Jacksonville Jaguars, I am very excited to continue in this role as I have the opportunity to lead and influence some great young men. Recently, God has brought greater clarity and purpose to my calling as a coach and, ultimately, as a teacher of men. The reality is this: those of us who coach young men and women, regardless of sport and age, are teachers. Now, more than ever, I have become keenly aware of the tremendous opportunity and responsibility set before me. I suppose age and maturity have played a part in my growing awareness. But it is also related to the fact that I have grown in my relationship with Christ; I know he is speaking to me and I am hearing him more clearly than ever. Certainly, God has richly blessed me, but with that blessing comes a wonderful responsibility to fulfill his calling.

He uses all life's experiences to prepare me for fulfilling his highest designs for me as a husband, father, friend, son and coach. I'm not sure if being asked to write this preface was my being called on or "called out", but I do know that, as a proud Catholic man with a beautiful wife and four healthy, happy children, God wants me to stand up for him, for my faith, for my family and, in many ways, just to stand up!

In today's world where the Internet and television are constantly bombarding us with the wrong messages, questions about values are being asked daily. Our children are being exposed to the secular and materialistic world at unprecedented levels. This is a critical time when, as a society, success is defined as the collection of material wealth and personal fame.

I recently spoke at a local high school in Florida and one of the questions asked by a young lady during the Q & A session had to do with happiness. The point I was trying to make was that real happiness was not the result money and material items. From this, the young lady asked, how could I possibly say that having a lot of money didn't make me happy? What else is there? Her question was very thought provoking and continues to disturb me. How can we stand by and watch mainstream society do only what is convenient and place importance on money and "things" and then wonder why, in many ways, the fabric of our culture is deteriorating? This is something we all need to think about and be prepared to face.

The way I can address these issues is through my coaching profession. I do feel God called me to be a coach and I am grateful to Him for the privilege. Coaches are teachers and teachers instruct youth. We must recognize the opportunity we have to impact the lives of our athletes, both on and off the field and in and out of the classroom. The world needs champions, "true champions". Remember our parents, teachers and coaches. These were the people who impacted our lives, provided positive examples and stood up for and protected us; they were our champions. Now, it is our turn to fill this role for today's children. And, we need to keep in mind that actions really do speak louder than words. What we teach, we must live. Whether we realize it or not, our athletes listen to us, but they watch us even more closely.

We are all charged with becoming that coach or teacher that makes a difference. Have courage, live with passion, attack each day with renewed enthusiasm, persevere throughout it all and do the right things for the right reasons. Our children will see this and learn to do the same. Avoid nothingness, life is full of meaning and goodness and we need to share it with others. We know life is about more than just personal gain; it is not all about collecting material possessions nor achieving victory at any cost. Now, we need for our children to know this as well. We need virtuous men and women to provide positive examples. As coaches we have that opportunity. As this book suggests, teaching virtues will actually help you maximize the abilities of your team. Humility, courage, discipline, work ethic, leadership, thankfulness are all characteristics that would benefit any team on the field. When we teach these to our teams, it transfers to daily life and shapes these young men and women into truly successful people on and off the field.

I encourage you to answer the call which is put forth by Pope Benedict XVI as he described the relationship between St Paul the virtues in sport: "…many look up to you, not only for your noteworthy sporting achievements, but also for the virtues and values that are characteristics of your sport." Use your position as a coach to love your athletes and teach them how to live a successful and fulfilling life- a life in which they will grow into mature young men and women and pass these same lessons on to the next generation. Teach them how to be well prepared instruments for God's work and purpose.

St Paul makes it clear to us that faith is a grace and gift from God, but remaining faithful is a lifetime commitment. Rejecting your conscience will shipwreck the Divine will for what God has deemed for you in life. Therefore we must nourish our souls with the word of God, just as we nourish our muscles with exercise and food that gives the body strength. The soul has need of this in order to stand strong in this battle.

The martyrs and saints continue to be relevant for us as members of the one true church. They teach us that standing for the truth is not only often inconvenient but it also has even cost them their lives. In fact, St Sebastian -the patron Saint of athletes- who was a captain in the Praetorian Guard of Emperor Diocletian kept the faith firmly despite persecution, trial, torture, and ultimately, martyrdom.

Yes, "all things work for good for those who love God" (Rom 8:28). And Paul continues: "What then shall we say to this? If God is for us, who can be against us? What will separate us from the love of Christ? Will anguish, or distress, or persecution, or famine, or nakedness, or peril, or the sword?. (…) No, in all these things we conquer overwhelmingly through him who loved us" (Rom 8: 32, 36, 38).

But we also must collaborate with him. Christ wants us to be prepared and well-trained so we can go forth fortified by Jesus Himself. What follows is a mini-training manual. This book succinctly charts a "course for champions"- a path already tread by the martyrs and the saints who have gone before us, and especially by St Paul. Not only his writings but Paul's very life shines before us as a path to be followed whether as a coach, a player or a committed Christian who wants to fight the good fight by conquering evil through good and winning the eternal victory.

Coach Jack Del Rio

INTRODUCTION

Do not let evil defeat you, instead, conquer evil with good.

Rom 12: 21

This is the "big match" that St Paul has entrusted to us. It seems like a tough contest, and it is! To conquer evil with good is the challenge of our time and each one of us is called to this – even those in the world of sport.

Such a great challenge reminds us of the need to have goals, to break out of our daily routine, to overcome our laziness and mediocrity. This may be uncomfortable for us, but such is demanded by excellence. Conquering evil through good marks a course for champions; it sets us on a path to eradicate our miserly selfishness, our excessive obsession with comfort and other unacceptable compromises with egoism.

As we tend to be normal people, we easily convince ourselves that we are satisfied with what we have and where we are at. We are good people who help out in the parish and with the youth whenever it is convenient, provided that we don't have to go against the flow or get too involved. A sort of "complacent mediocrity" is the path to which we are all inclined. Yet, in this way, we run the risk of just getting by while not realizing how we are "are wretched, pitiable, poor, blind, and naked" (Rev 3:17). And then we ask ourselves "What happened? How come so many young people have 'lost it'?" It seemed like everything was going so well...

In stark contrast to this life of complacency stands the life of the apostle Paul. St Paul invites us to engage in the battle: to fight, to be courageous, to put ourselves on the line. His words today continue to resound as a stumbling block, removing the very ground from under our feet and forcing us to evaluate everything anew, and not leaving us at ease. St John Chrysostom touches on the secret of St Paul when he says:

> Paul shows us in a very particular way, what it is to be human, the nobility of our nature, and the strength of this thinking being. Day by day he aimed ever higher; each day he rose up with greater zeal and with a new eagerness faced the dangers that threatened him. (John Chrysostom, Homily on St Paul: PG 50, 478)

Citius, altius, fortius is the famous phrase that expresses in short the spirit of the Olympic Games. 'Faster, higher, stronger' means refusing mediocrity, living with passion and excellence, not holding anything back and giving your all. St Paul reveals this 'Olympic' attitude when he said:

> Forgetting what lies behind and straining forward to what lies ahead, I press on toward the goal for the prize of the heavenly call of God in Christ Jesus. (Phil 3: 14)

We also must climb higher every day towards the loftiest peaks with increased strength and passion. We also are called to live our faith in Christ with this spirit of *citius, altius, fortius* – as we should strive for greater perfection both on and off the field.

By taking a closer look at the life of St Paul and his sport metaphors, this book seeks to help us to distil from them some valuable lessons on the virtues that are as valid for sport as they are for daily life. In doing so, we seek to assist parents and instructors – but especially coaches – in passing on this perennial wisdom to their young people so that they can live these sports virtues in all areas of their lives.

We hope that this simple course for champions, enlightened by St Paul, can be reference and guide for all those in sports who do not want to be "defeated by evil", but rather, who seek "to conquer evil with good!" (Rom 12: 21).

CHAPTER 1

SAINT PAUL: AN 'OLYMPIC' APOSTLE

I have fought the good fight, I have finished the race,
I have kept the faith.

2 Tim 4: 7

The popularity of sport in Paul's time allowed this competitive terminology to enter the vocabulary of daily life, and in particular that of the classroom. In the so called 'gymnasium' of the Hellenic culture, sport as well as academic studies represented the training ground for young people.

We can find athletic metaphors in the philosophy of his time. Cicero used to praise the boxer for the virtue of fortitude, while Seneca often compared the athlete with the philosopher, considering the athlete as the one with the best endurance due to his intensive training and asceticism. (Asceticism is derived from the Greek word *asksis* and signifies the intense physical training and discipline endured by an athlete. We also find analogies that with sport in the ancient Jewish world in the writings of the Jewish philosopher Philo of Alexandria.

Until St Paul, no sacred writer in the Bible had referred to competitive sport with such rigor and precision. So we find ourselves asking: "Why Paul?" Some biblical scholars think that Paul's reference to sport was only a way of imitating the typical rhetoric of his day where sport metaphors were an integral part of moral dialogue of the Stoics. But a closer look at these metaphors through the eyes of a sportsperson reveals to us a man who possessed not only technical knowledge about sport, but also something of the *agon* spirit.

We know very little about the athletic competitions of ancient Tarsus, but the famous Isthmian Games in Corinth, comparable to the Olympic Games, certainly offered Paul a variety of rich sports analogies with which he could attract the attention of simple people and explain the Christian life in an understandable way. In fact, the sports terminology so often found in his writings seems to suggest that the Apostle to the Gentiles was certainly familiar with athletic training. So, besides the Judaic tradition, Paul drew upon concepts, images, terminology, expressions as well as philosophical and literary elements from Hellenism and its world of sport, to take Christ's message to everybody. Although St Paul doesn't speak about sport in order to advance any kind of theology of sport, he was attentive to reading the signs of the time.

Indeed Paul's attitude towards sport, far from being one of rejection or avoidance, was actually marked by a sense of respect and esteem. As the sporting Pope, John Paul II, stated in his homily during the International Jubilee of Sport in 1984:

> Paul knew, therefore, the fundamental value of sport, not only as an element of comparison to show a superior ethic and ascetic ideal, but also in its intrinsic reality of coefficient for human formation and part of his culture and civilization. (April 12, 1984)

But, we dare to suggest a further reason to explain why we often find competitive references in his writings. Paul highly esteemed athletic competition because he himself, in his mental, spiritual and physical attitude, "breathed" an Olympic spirit, as he himself wanted to be a champion for Christ's cause. In what sense?

He always aspired to greater things. He wanted to preach in more places and to more people, to the extent that he was ready to put off his ultimate encounter with the Lord in order to bring more followers closer to the cause of Christ. In fact, let's have a look at his "record breaking" *Curriculum Vitae:*

> I think that I am not in any way inferior to these 'super apostles.'[…] Are they ministers of Christ? I am talking like a madman--I am a better one: with far greater labors, far more imprisonments, with countless floggings, and often near death. Five times I have received from the Jews the forty lashes minus one. Three times I was beaten with rods. Once I received a stoning. Three times I was shipwrecked; for a night and a day I was adrift at sea; on frequent journeys, in danger from rivers, danger from bandits, danger from my own people, danger from Gentiles, danger in the city, danger in the wilderness, danger at sea, danger from false brothers and sisters; in toil and hardship, through many a sleepless night, hungry and thirsty, often without food, cold and naked. (2 Cor 11:5; 23 - 27)

We can also reflect on the many kilometers he walked, the sufferings he bore and obstacles he overcame. This man, short in stature, but possessing an iron will, has become a champion of the Christian faith!

Additionally, Paul knew how to put into practice other virtues typical of an athlete such as courage, perseverance, endurance, focus, willpower, commitment and team spirit. Since Paul's time, the popularity of sport has not diminished. On the contrary, it is continually increasing. In our globalized world, sport has become a significant phenomenon that, with its universal language, can virtually unite the whole planet around a World Cup or another international competition.

Especially today, the world has great need of true champions, people like St Paul who are capable of facing the challenges of life with energy and enthusiasm. Therefore, it seems right to explore this link between the genuine mentality of an athlete and the life of the apostle Paul. On one hand, this will help sport itself to be enlightened by the example of St Paul and regain its ability to contribute to the formation of the person and be an integral part of culture and society. On the other hand, the dynamism of sport will give us a new perspective in appreciating the greatness of this 'Olympic' apostle and the greatness of our proper Christian vocation within the world of sport. Paul has "fought the good fight, he has finished the race, he has kept the faith"… Now it's our turn.

CHAPTER 2

EDUCATING THROUGH SPORT

To build up the body of Christ, …until we all form the perfect man, fully mature with the fullness of Christ himself.

Eph 4: 13

Sport is one of humanity's greatest assets. It reproduces, in a symbolic way, the reality of life with all of its fatigue, fighting, suffering, desperation, anger, joy, satisfaction and happiness.

When participating in sport, whether professional or amateur, every match is a challenge. We can win or lose, but the beauty of sport exists in the fact that every defeat is never final. We can always muster the strength for another challenge, another opportunity.

The ability to compete, to win and lose, turning defeat into a means of challenging ourselves, is as valid to our daily lives as it is to sport. Technique, preparation, study, tenacity, pursuit of excellence, training, continuous game plan revision, rethinking, updating and perfecting …all of these are part and parcel of sport as well as daily life and work. And all have the same unique objective of preparing for the 'game', and equipping us for victory. Sometimes we lose and feel like dieing, other times we win and feel over the moon. This is part of the game, this is part of life.

Growth and development through sport

Millions of young people worldwide have grown into adults and become better citizens through playing sports. Some of them have become great champions. Sports, alongside the family, the school and the parish have for many generations played a real educational role in building a true community.

John Paul II himself entrusted Catholic sports associations with a great mission: that of going beyond the mere promotion of sport so as to also contribute to answering the fundamental questions the new generations are asking about the meaning of life, its purpose and its goal (*Cf.* Address to the Italian Sports Center, June 26, 2004). At the same time he offers us the key to interpret the real role of sport today and throughout human history: *to teach the value of life.*

To educate through sport is neither easy nor predictable. It takes patience and sacrifice. Every commitment, every way that aims to develop the person and offer hope in place of despair, requires constant effort. It's hard to create and provide an activity plan that establishes sport as a serious thing amongst the serious things of life as it takes effort to develop quality sports activities that can really contribute to transforming today's youth into the real assets for tomorrow.

Sports activity is truly an educational process if it produces meaningful relationships, promotes social links, encourages holistic wellbeing and assists the athlete in the development of self-knowledge and the formation of his own personality. Sports are also educational when they are capable of welcoming everyone: the skilful and the less skilful, the able-bodied and the handicapped, the last as well as the first.

Sport as a reflection of our competitive society

Today's sports continue to possess an attraction and inherent dynamism of such power that they can excite the senses and emotions of millions of people of any age in a fully engaging and totally surprising ways. The 'power' of sport is widely manifest in people's everyday circumstances of work, daily relationships and in how they shape their lifestyles and citizenship.

After all, it's worth noticing how the dominant model of sport today also conforms to the society in which we live, that is based on consumerism, and success under the guise of appearance and with extensive support from the media. In this way sport aligns itself to the standards typical of winning cultures, which seem straight forward on the outside, but are actually complex and sophisticated in terms of the way they access and build personal and social success.

It's no coincidence that sport becomes more and more a reflection of a competitive, agnostic, amoral, selfish society that is void of aims. Sport, influenced by this society, adopts its philosophy and obtains its results. Consequently it promotes only "number one" and considers all the rest as insignificant and marginal unless they can be used in serving some rhetorical purpose. This approach fuels a type of sport marked by an ambivalence that generates conflicting conditions and is prone to many ethical risks.

Anthropological crisis

Particularly in difficult times as these, it becomes essential to rethink our values and ask what gives real purpose and meaning to our lives. It is necessary to determine the guiding principles and how to witness them. Something similar is taking place in professional sport, which on one hand is subject to the principles of finance and entertainment but on the other hand is deeply in crisis, having lost sight of the concerns and questions that had always given sport its meaning, such as… What type of person are we seeking to develop through sports? What values are we promoting? To what extent do our sporting activities serve as a "school of life" in helping individuals to grow?

Unfortunately the causes of this crisis are mainly of an ethical and anthropological nature. Seeking success at any cost leads to foul play, corruption, deceit, and the desire to prevail against opponents with any means whatsoever, to the point of resorting to doping and steroids in order to gain the advantage. There's no shortage of sociologists who claim that the fame, wealth and power which are imposed as the "new values" in professional sport will end up conditioning the lives of young people. Other experts claim that sports are losing its values altogether.

Such a crisis requires that all involved – managers, athletes, coaches, supporters, sponsors, doctors, pharmacists, journalists, educators and administrators, make a serious examination of conscience in order to re-establish an ethical and moral code. But, if there's an absence of basic obligations towards others, in terms of loyalty and honesty, and towards oneself to the point of risking life through taking certain medications, then we have to ask ourselves… Where are we starting out from? On which principles should we base an ethical code? Who has the moral authority to even suggest it?

What type of person do we want to develop?

The great cultural challenge of our time is to re-determine clearly what type of person and what type of civil society we want to develop through sport. In the particular case of Italy –with its parish based sports clubs– the Catholic Church built and promoted a unique sport system because they had a very clear idea of the type of person they wanted to nurture and the type of civil society they wanted to build through sporting activity. Today, we are called to launch, with the same clarity of purpose, a new sports and educational plan that determines the guidelines for the sport culture of the twenty first century.

Sport has always spoken through the language of the heart. Big national and international events have always generated collective emotions. They have fulfilled the instinct and the desire for well being of millions of people. But market forces have greatly conditioned this valuable vehicle of humanity by confining it within the temporal logic of the entertainment and business world. All values have been sacrificed in the name of profit, personal interests and victory at any cost. We no longer make use of sport; on the contrary sport uses us, reducing us to a mere commodity.

Today sport needs the intervention of a new humanism. What people want from sport, especially young people, is above all for it to give meaning to their lives. Before the need for pure physical activity, there is a need for life, love and happiness; there is a need for a safe haven from fear and deceit. In this way sports activity becomes a creative resource for building personality, behavior, communication skills, relationships, and a sense of belonging and real community.

We should start from asking ourselves some simple questions: "What's the purpose of sport?" "What type of person are we trying to provide a service for in modern society?" And in our case "What role should sport assume within our society?" It's enough to simply ask these questions to understand that any effort from institutions and the sports world must not be reduced to a search for champions and records, and that mass sport cannot keep growing in a savage way but needs guidance and not simply funding.

Great attention should be dedicated to encourage those activities whose principles guarantee the development of the educational purpose of sport. Always bearing in mind that this purpose cannot be separated from a valid social context, which is exactly the opposite aim of today's gym workouts activity, where sport increasingly tends to be solitary.

Giving meaning to life through sport

Our great task is precisely that of offering -through quality sports activities that are capable of generating a real experience of life- a radical alternative to the mediocrity, the sense of emptiness, the vacuum of values and the 'nothingness' that stifles us. Educational work is valid only if we base our educational activities on serious values when it comes to facing and resolving the issues that are necessarily raised today. In other words, ethical relativism must be overcome in order to make education possible.

In sport, our relationship with young people must have the aim of building communities. Educating youth is a collective responsibility that cannot be delegated to the family alone, which today is in constant change, increasingly fragile and becoming weaker and weaker. Neither can it be just left to the teacher or the school. It's a collective responsibility.

This 'nothingness' is equivalent to a life without meaning. It's a life that is content with half-measures and banalities. It's a life without expectations, without hope. This pervasive 'nothingness' hangs over us all in many shapes and forms. We all run the risk of conceding to a 'nothingness' that withers us away at the core, because we don't choose 'nothingness', we simply abandon ourselves to it. In fact, to not have a clear goal is to succumb to this nothingness for without a clear goal how can we grow or make progress?

The opposite of this nothingness is a fullness of life: "I came so that they might have life and have it more abundantly" (Jn 10: 11). Christ is the goal as well as the way.. Like St Paul, we must press on towards the goal. Paul begs his readers to imitate him and he imitates Christ We must grow and mature, assisting others along the way, until we all "form the perfect man, fully mature with the fullness of Christ himself" (Eph 4:13).

As we will see in the following chapters, the Christian anthropology of St Paul offers a notable contribution to sports ethics along two paths. First, by fostering athletes and managers that live according to virtues. Secondly, by enabling them to discern between what is good for the sound development of the athlete from any evil that could emerge.

CHAPTER 3

OUTDOING OTHERS IN GOODNESS

Let love be sincere; hate what is evil, hold on to what is good;
love one another with mutual affection;
outdo one another in showing them respect.

Rm 12: 9-10

It's a great competition, isn't it? It is great because it frees us from our pride, it breaks down our superiority complexes and fills us with peace and serenity. Unfortunately this particular sport –that of outdoing others in showing them respect– is not practiced very much.

The scramble for first place in order to be seen, heard, considered, applauded, and awarded is now so culturally rooted in our being that it has become difficult to eradicate. Everyone likes to compete, but there is one competition that, at first sight, is not so attractive... though when participating in it, it becomes more and more fascinating and ends up being appreciated more than any other. This is the challenge of putting the other first, of striving to "outdo" the other in showing them respect.

Yet, we might wonder "Why should I do this?" Our adopted commercial logic tells us that this is a deception, an injustice, it tells us to always place ourselves first. Yet, it is not self-indulgence, but rather, self-giving that will quench that deeper thirst for joy and for the infinite that is within us. We are all called to enter this competition. Just imagine if each one of us would strive to put the other first before ourselves … a mysterious miracle would take place. Each one of us would experience the inner peace that we all seek, but seldom know how to achieve it.

Here are five ways we can place the other first: through welcoming, guiding, training, accompanying and giving hope to those entrusted to their care. These are five fundamental actions that every educator, parent, teacher –but especially every coach– must exercise in order to help a young person gain a sense and purpose to their existence.

Welcoming

We live in a "disposable" age where things only have value when they serve one's personal interests and afterwards they are immediately discarded…In fact, think of how often this mentality can carry over to work relationships, friendships and even marriage! The art of "welcoming" a person -regardless of what benefit they might bring me- is an action that definitely goes against the flow.

Welcoming is gratuitous; it brings our heart into play and makes every relationship significant because it gives meaning to relationships beyond the logic of selfish profit. In fact, real communities can only be built through this type of meaningful relationships that imply solidarity; otherwise they will be for mere personal interest, a form of mere trading in relationships with others.

Welcoming implies responsibility. Welcoming a person is my *response* to the gift of the person who comes into my life. Establishing this new relationships requires this personal initiative of my response. Every new relationship sets in motion a process of change in both the other person and myself, making us both responsible for this new venture. We cannot pretend that nothing in me has changed. Recall in the story of *The Little Prince* how the initial dialogue with the fox sparks a beautiful friendship that is nurtured over time through subsequent visits. We too are responsible for the friendships we begin and we can't go backwards, as that would make us less of a person or hypocrites. It is up to us to fan into flame and to start again, a thousand times if necessary, in order to give new meaning and depth to human relationships.

This is precisely this kind of human relationship that will change these peoples' lives. That's why we say that welcoming is a process that opens a door to experiencing life, because only these real human experiences change people's lives. It certainly won't be trophies or medals that will change the life of a young boy. Rather, it will be the personal experiences which he —or even a young man or coach for that matter- has gained through his sports team or athletic club that will remain with him forever as beautiful and determining moments in his life. In this way, the sports club will represent the educational place that helped him to grow as a person, and not just an empty place… without memories.

Human relationships, therefore ought to be at the heart of sporting activity. Sports that are viewed as a mere exchange of goods, where one passes by reception, pays, plays and then goes home, serve no purpose: they are a waste of time!

Guiding

Guiding is fantastic and difficult work as it requires helping young people to build fulfilling ways to become adults. However, guiding doesn't mean telling a boy or girl what to do, nor does it mean organizing their life. Guiding means helping them to reactivate and reorganize their cognitive, emotional and key energies, so as to plan their lives in a structured way, avoiding getting trapped in the mediocrity of this world. It is necessary to help them to take back control of their lives and determine the meaning of their existence. Our task is saving young people from meaninglessness, from living life in a passive way, from being trapped into harmful lifestyles and the modern marketing's illusions.

The seriousness of today's educational crisis demands from us quality sport activity that can accompany young people in becoming adults. The mechanism of the switch from adolescence to adulthood has jammed. Today we lack rites of passage. We are left only with one age...the perennial teenager. Yet, we ask: why doesn't a young person want to become an adult? In the past we couldn't wait to become adults, there was excitement. But today perhaps things have changed as it seems that young people don't find in us the role models, the credible witnesses, or the harbingers of the high ideals for which committing oneself to, fighting for and dedicating their lives to is worthwhile.

Becoming an adult is hard work. To be adult means to have emotional and economic stability. It takes effort... so, for some, they think it is better to not even start! Yet for many others- for millions of young people, sport is this start as it is an opportunity to begin to give some structure and stability to their lives.

Often we give young people opportunities but we don't help them to plan their lives in a structured way. Guiding means helping a young person to plan his life using every opportunity, sport, group experiences and anything else that a sports team can offer.

Training

The third action is that of training. We are experts at this! Yet we often limit ourselves to training only our body and our physical abilities, or refining our sports techniques, but this is not enough. As we said at the outset, ability and technique are not everything.

First of all we need to help the youth train their hearts. Training the heart implies training desire- that ability, that mysterious force, that curiosity in ourselves that leads us to be seekers of a clear goal... It is desire that triggers this search! If sport fails to train our desire, it's just a muscular exercise.

If a boy who plays sport is not able to improve his life beyond technical results, for that boy the sport experience will be a failure from an educational point of view. If we keep our heart out of sport, the educational process is incomplete, corrupted and loses its significance. The heart brings passion into play. Of course this passion needs to be controlled an channel by our will, but with out this emotion sport is cold and lifeless.

A training in effort is also required because I will not achieve anything unless I work and sweat, unless I give my best, unless I try and try again ten thousand times. Effort is at the heart of training, at the heart of competition, at the heart of anything related to sport, as well as anything that is worthy or enduring in this life, because life is tough, life is sacrifice, life is, at times, an uphill race! The very idea of effort has been conveniently made to disappear from educational vocabulary. As a trainer or coach, the words "effort", "sacrifice and difficulty" must be part of our vocabulary as they are significant elements of every educational course.

It is also necessary to train young people to face difficulties in order to overcome them. Everyone must be willing to take risks and strive to overcome mistakes. Mistakes ought not to be seen as something negative, but rather positive, as they are at the foundation of every progression and improvement. Training young people to overcome mistakes means helping them to strengthen their own lives from within, so that when a young person makes a mistake or faces difficulties, he or she won't jump out of a window. Rather, they will have the ability and inner strength to get back in the game and start over again. This is the real work of a teacher!

We also need to help train the youth in happiness by teaching them that happiness is not something that we buy nor simply happens by chance. Happiness is a goal; it is an achievement. Teaching youth to believe in a greater good regardless of their present circumstances is also the task of a coach. There are too many prophets of doom out there, capable of seeing the wrong in others without ever being able to see it in themselves.

We must be positive in our outlook. To believe in good regardless of apparent circumstances means not to fear evil. Evil will always be there because it's no abstract entity, it's real. However, the good exists too. It's up to us to be bearers of goodness. We must keep in mind that evil acts through us only when we cooperate with it.

Lastly, a training in confidence. It's necessary to not loose confidence and to transmit confidence even though we may meet people along the way that often turn out to be different from what we first thought. We need to have and show faith in them even when they make mistakes.

Accompanying

The fourth action is that of accompanying: keeping an attentive eye on the youth within our care; staying close. It's a difficult job that is no longer practiced. Accompanying means to be a 'companion' on the way, walking part of the way together.

A young person needs an adult that says: "Go for it! Fight for it! Give it all you've got! Don't worry. I'm here if you need anything." Often it's not even necessary to be physically present, it's enough for a young person to just know that he is not alone and that someone's there, that there is an adult in his life that cares for him. Even though they don't want to admit it, they need to feel that someone cares for them. Today the widespread sense of unhappiness among young people is the result of a generation of adults that doesn't bother to say "How are you? I am here, don't worry! Don't be afraid, keep going! Try your best, fight on, sweat it out! Try again! I am with you!"

Accompanying is a silent presence…it's not a presence made out of talks, judgments, or offering a list of "do's and don'ts". Accompanying is a subtle activity. Yet the youth, with their acute sensitivity, perceive it and appreciate it.

Accompanying is a type of apprenticeship we offer the youth. Yet, this apprenticeship doesn't mean only learning a trade, like how to become a goldsmith or a football player, but learning how to become an adult. Becoming an adult requires an apprenticeship because being adult is a difficult task. True accompanying means helping the other person to believe in himself, because when an adult is interested in a young person, the latter gains a sense of self-confidence.

Accompanying is the discrete, yet authoritative and significant presence of an adult who, with an affirming glance, can guide a young life in its development. It's a difficult responsibility, but it is the responsibility of a real educator. As managers, coaches, parents, teachers, or priests, we must rediscover the art of exercising this significant presence with youth in our lives. Yet, as we know, it takes more than just a glance: this is the difficult job of witnessing through our actions by being valid role models. We often say beautiful things with words, but our actions and behaviors undermine us. Accompanying is also a moral as well as a pedagogical and cultural challenge. It requires loyalty.

Giving hope

The fifth action is that of transmitting hope. In this we truly perform our Christian role. Giving hope means building hope, a constructive hope that gives us all the strength to carry on when everyone else gives up. Keeping our head up when everything seems to fail. Coping with educational failures and starting all over again when everyone else runs away from responsibility...

Hope is a type of educational charity. The great youth educator, St Don Bosco, reminded his fellow Salesian priests that it is not enough that young people be loved....they also need to realize that they are loved by our actions! This is part of the charism we have received from him, that of educating youth with our very lives, displaying the values we believe in. Hope enables us to refresh the too often empty well of the human heart with love.

Yet, developing the very source of hope is the real foundation that will support all other actions. As Pope Benedict XVI stated in *Spe Salvi*, his encyclical on hope:

> It is true that anyone who does not know God, even though he may entertain all kinds of hopes, is ultimately without hope, without the great hope that

sustains the whole of life (cf. Eph 2:12). Man's great, true hope which holds firm in spite of all disappointments can only be God — God who has loved us and who continues to love us... (n. 27)

In the end, it is a Person who enables us to be joyful in hope.

Chapter 4

SPORT VIRTUES

Imitate me, then, just as I imitate Christ.

1 Cor 11: 1

Practice makes perfect! This is a phrase frequently used in relation to young people and especially in sports environments. This expression helps to motivate those who have little patience in front of the discipline of training. In fact, latent in these words of wisdom is a profound anthropology that considers each person's great potential as something to be developed little by little. Each of us can improve our skills, actions and behavior. But, not in an instant; rather, through the continual repetition of his actions.

Sport disciplines are practiced and performed with minute attention to detail in order to be perfected, and this is precisely what distinguishes this play from that of running around the play ground at recess. Let's consider, for example, shooting a three-pointer in basketball. Given the great distance from the three point line to the basket, it takes a lot of training to master a three-point shot. First one has to strengthen the arm muscle by repetition. Then, after every attempt, it's necessary to analyze what went right and what went wrong. This routine is repeated umpteen times until accuracy is achieved… and even then practice must continue on a daily basis until the technique becomes a natural reflex.

A similar dynamic also occurs in our behavior off court. While some instinctive actions are beyond our immediate control, others, such as our behavior, our attitude towards ourselves and others, depends on the decisions of our will, even if we feel swayed by our emotions and feelings. Through the repetition of our freely determined actions we choose to develop either good or bad habits.

In the moral field, we can use the word virtue to express the habits that have been strengthen through the repetition of good actions that consequently facilitates the exercise of other good action. As the philosopher Aristotle observed some 25 centuries ago: we acquire the virtues by first exercising them as also happens in the case of the arts.... So too we become just by doing just acts, temperate by doing temperate acts, brave by doing brave acts (*Nichomachaen Ethics*, Bk. II, 1). In this way, these acquired human virtues become fixed behaviors.

So just like acquiring the habit of shooting a three pointer, it is also necessary to perfect our human actions through practice. In doing so, these virtues provide self-control and stability in leading a morally good life.

Whereas the Latin word *virtus* literally means 'virility' and carries connotations of valor and manliness, the Greek equivalent for virtue, on the other hand, is the word *arête* and means excellence, or literally 'way of being perfect'. This implies that a virtue helps us to excel in something and to act in the best possible way. For the Ancient Greeks, virtue is a goal to be reached as it is human perfection at its best: excellence!

Because people who practice sports tend to seek to improve and in this way strive for excellence, it seems that sports might have an inherent and reciprocal relationship with virtue. In fact, Pope Benedict XVI noted in his address to civil authorities during his visit to Prague how sports offer the young people an opportunity to excel. So, the Holy Father went on to ask: "Is it not equally true that when presented with high ideals they will also aspire to moral virtue and a life of compassion and goodness?" (September 26, 2009). The Holy Father is implying that the quest for excellence in sport should also be applied to the pursuit of moral virtue. But we can also ask, what about some of the moral virtues themselves… could they also not be trained and perfected in the practice of a sport?

Way back in 1955, Pope Pius XII already gave us a positive response to this question in his address to a Catholic sports association:

> Sports education wants to introduce young people to the formation of its virtues, these are among others: honesty which prevents deceit; docility and obedience to the wise direction of the team leader; a spirit of sacrifice when necessary to deny oneself for the sake of the club; commitment to engagements; modesty in victory; generosity towards losers; serenity when things go wrong; patience towards the demanding public; fairness if competitive sport is linked to freely agreed financial interests; chastity in general and temperance, recommended by the ancients. Although all these virtues concern the physical and external nature, they are, in fact, Christian virtues, that cannot be fully obtained without an intimate religious spirit and, we can add, without frequent prayer (October 9, 1955).

He went on to state that nobody expects two separate independent lists, one for the virtues of the Christian and another for the sportsperson, because they both permeate and integrate each other.

Then the categorical question is: "Can sport be considered an activity that develops human virtues in a reasonable and consistent way?" Our answer to this question is a whole-hearted 'yes!', but it is not affirmed without the inclusion of certain conditions.

Through the opportunities sports affords to order one's passions and behavior in line with reason and will, and especially through its repetition, it can help to develop virtues. But, it should be noted that sport is only one discipline, amongst many others, such as practicing a musical instrument, for example, that can help with the formation of virtues.

Secondly, the formation of virtues as an outcome is not a foregone conclusion. It will depend upon how sport is promoted, managed and played. There are some other conditions too: the supremacy of the human being above any sports activity for example, that must be always respected and guaranteed.

Another condition is the sport environment. Children learn more by example than by verbal teaching. "Imitate me, then, just as I imitate Christ" (1 Cor 11:1) said St Paul. Virtue starts at home, and begins in sport with the coach himself. Are we examples for the youth of what we demand form them? Unfortunately, we know that many professional athletes do not offer the young people great examples to follow. In light of what has been said, someone could ask himself: "If sports form virtue, why do we have so many athletes, especially at a professional level, that don't consistently reflect these human virtues on the field?" Here we need to make some remarks.

First of all we need to point out that bad behavior creates a stir while exemplary behavior often passes unnoticed. Secondly, there is the previously mentioned problem that the formation of virtues through sports practice is conditioned by human freedom and by the way the training is organized. Human virtues are just that, human, because they imply the exercise of our free will and can never be automatically ensured.

Despite this, and without empirical evidence, we continue to make the claim that the practice of sport among young people, and above all team sport, offers a great opportunity to form the human qualities of teamwork, obeying the rules, appreciate and practicing fair play and self-improvement. Sport offers repetitive opportunities to stimulate the formation of so many human virtues that are useful both on and off the field of play.

Finally, it's worth remembering that the great philosophers used to believe that to be truly virtuous it is necessary to pursue all the virtues. In sport, like in other disciplines, it is not possible to master any specific virtue without simultaneously improving the rest of them. For example, in sport, without the virtue of discipline it's very difficult to gain self-control. So, whoever wants to be truly virtuous must pursue every virtue. In the following chapters, we have chosen some human virtues as based upon St Paul's writings, namely, respecting the body, discipline, knowing how to behave in victory, knowing how to behave in defeat, teamwork and perseverance. Yet, in speaking about these specifically, it is not easy to isolate them from others as they are all interconnected.

Chapter 5

Respect for the Body

Do you not realize that your body is the temple of the Holy Spirit,
who is in you and whom you received from God? ...
So use your body for the glory of God.

1Cor. 6: 19-20

Sculptured bodies, strong bodies, perpetually young bodies, exposed bodies, hidden bodies, provocative bodies, disposable bodies, bodies on a diet, bodies on drugs, bodies that are cared for, bodies that are neglected; bodies that reveal a family resemblances and bodies that tell us stories of sadness or joy.

We have entered a post-modern era in which our body has become a machine. If we believe that our body is a mere object, then it is easy to convince ourselves that the person is also a mere object. An object is used for something, and after using it, it is either disposed of or recycled. Unfortunately, the same also happens with the subject- the human person.

We all run the serious risk of considering the other person as having value only in view of our personal interests and advantages...we use them and then throw them. This occurs in work relationships, in friendships... even in marriage. The same thing also happens to a lot of men and women in sport, where their body is used, bought or sold to the highest bidder, subjected to all sorts of pills and injections, and then discarded.

Each one of us, indeed, is an 'animated' body, a body with a soul and full of tensions and passions for life. Through this body we think, love, express ourselves, communicate and hope. For this reason an education towards respect for the body is based on our recognition, appreciation and acceptance of our bodily existence.

The body as the window to the person

Our body is like the foyer to the other dimensions of our being. A room needs to let in air and light to give space to life, it also needs to be linked to other rooms in order to be in relation with them. From this foyer we begin to perceive and learn to grasp the essence of the world itself. A child, through his own body and especially through physical activity, begins to recognize himself and relate to others, coming into contact with a wider and wider horizon of life and meaning.

The body is the window to the person. Our face is said to be the mirror of the soul, it reveals our feelings and moods, in fact, all our body speaks of what happens within us, our posture, our attitude towards reality, the way we relate to others, our inner feelings towards diversity… Our body is the custodian of our uniqueness: in our DNA, in our finger prints, in the pupil of our eyes…there will never be another like myself. Through our body we express who we are and what we think of life.

The human body has always provoked deep questions about who we are: "What is my body?" "Am I my body?" "What can I do with it?" These are crucial questions and, if left unanswered, they will keep us enslaved to the current culture and its tendencies. Our body lives the adventure of being born and dieing, growing and aging, eating, rejoicing and suffering. The history of each one of us, with its expectations and hopes, sacrifices and sorrows, victories and defeats, is all written and played out in our body. My body defines me, limits me. It is always at the centre of my world. My body is something that I can touch, see, sense. It is awaiting and anxious. It is searching. What is it searching for? Its identity and truth!. Our body is not something we can dispose of when we want, therefore if we abuse it, this will have an effect on our person and harm even the truth about ourselves. A healthy approach that teaches us to respect our body in contained in the following principle: "Care of the body, yes. Cult of the body, no!".

When we play sport it is especially our body that speaks. Our gestures, facial expressions, shouts of joy or pain... are all ways of communicating.

Some body expressions are universal and have always the same meaning: laughing, for example, is a sign of happiness. Athletes use body language too. With their gestures and movements they express a great deal of emotions and feelings: love, pain, joy, regrets. The tired face of a long-distance runner reveals his effort and tenacity during the race. The discus thrower sometimes lets out a cry of satisfaction; that shout is not in English, Italian or Russian, it is a universal shout of joy! Even more important is what a sport person expresses with his bodily actions and behavior: fair play, respect of the rules, and respect for one's opponents.

The body in Christianity

People who blame the Church for not being concerned about the body and the culture of the physique are far from the truth, because they are the first ones who want to restrict the Church's competence to only 'purely spiritual' matters. On the contrary, the Church has always considered the human body as a masterpiece of creation in the material sphere. We find in St Paul a highly positive valuation of the body when, in his first letter to the Corinthians -a people known in the ancient world both for the underworld around the temple of Aphrodite and the Isthmic games- he writes:

> Do you not realize that your bodies are members of Christ's body; ...Do you not realize that your body is the temple of the Holy Spirit, who is in you and whom you received from God? You are not your own property then; you have been bought at a price. So use your body for the glory of God! (Cor. 6: 15; 19-20).

The human body is not only the masterpiece of creation, but also an integral part of the human person himself and temple of the Holy Spirit. In the same letter to the Corinthians he wrote: "Whatever you eat, or drink, and whatever else you do, do it all for the glory of God" (1 Cor 10: 31).

Sport is part of this "whatever else you do" mentioned by St Paul and it's certainly part of that "care of the body". In fact, not only can we glorify God in sport, we must! Therefore, sport should promote respect of the body and be instrumental to learning to understand its deepest needs, but not in order to put it at the disposal of the latest fashion or external pressures.

Taking care of our body will enable us to do better than just setting a record, sport can become a precious means to take care of ourselves and do our duties with more and more effectiveness. Exercising our body in a healthy way in order to rest our mind and prepare it for new tasks, to sharpen our senses, train our muscles for effort to strengthen the character and form the will. This is showing respect to our body as well as for the real sense of sport.

Relating with others through our body

Additionally, through our body we relate to others, we rejoice and suffer, we experience our own weaknesses as well as strengths. What's the point of beating a record by modifying the metabolism of our body? What's the point of forcing very young people to spend seven, eight hours a day in the gym just to gain victory?

Paul, trying to simplify the Greek way of thinking, which he knew very well, used to differentiate between the material part of humanity, the body, and the spiritual one. These two parts at times seemed to be diametrically opposed. Yet in the Jewish world, in which Paul was raised, the word 'body', instead was nearly non existent; they preferred to use the word *basar*, 'flesh'. In the Old Testament, the body doesn't appear as something independent, but always related to the whole. The body is the concrete point of man's *being in relation with* others: the body is the person himself, in time and space, in his (physical) being. For Paul the person is always 'placed' in time and space with his own features, story, context and culture.

As mentioned, it is through the body that the person enters into relationships with other people. It is interesting to re-read the passage of the letter to the Corinthians (6: 20) where Paul says: "Glorify God in your body" that is, in your *being in relation with others*. Paul's understanding of the human body and its social dimension helps us to better understand what he means when he says that the Church is the body of Christ.

To conclude this chapter, these words of Pope Benedict XV to a group of Olympic skiers sum up our thoughts in an excellent way:

> Body, spirit and soul form a single unity and each component must be in harmony with the other. You know how necessary this interior harmony is in order to reach sporting goals at the highest levels. Consequently, even the most demanding sports must be rooted in a holistic view of the human person, recognizing his profound dignity and favoring an overall development and full maturity of the person. (October 6, 2007).

Chapter 6

WILL POWER

Athletes exercise self-control in all things... I do not run aimlessly, nor do I box as though beating the air; but I punish my body and enslave it, so that ... I myself should not be disqualified.
1Cor. 9: 25-27

Ever since its modern inception in society, the Church has valued sport as an effective antidote to softness and lethargy. This is all the more relevant in today's world of instant gratifications, where nearly everything is accessible by clicking a computer icon, and where especially the youth are pampered in epidemic proportions! The "couch potato" has been replaced only by the "mouse potato" to signify the person who spends excessive hours every day vegetating in front of a computer screen without a definite aim or purpose. Apart from the negative consequences this can have on one's physical health, this widespread lethargy and lack of will power threaten human maturity because without a firm will a person becomes reduced to the status of a dead leaf -blown to and fro by the wind.

How can sport be an antidote to this softness of will? How can physical exercise strengthen one's will power and self-control? To help us answer this, let's take a closer look at the will power and determination of the Apostle Paul. In his first letter to the Corinthians he compares himself to an athlete who exercises self-control in all things:

I do not run aimlessly, nor do I box as though beating the air; but I punish my body and master it, so that after proclaiming to others, I myself should not be disqualified" (1Cor 9: 24-27).

Although Paul did not compete as an athlete in the Isthmus Games, he was undoubtedly a man accustomed to work and fatigue. By never relenting, enduring long and treacherous journeys, he manifests a sense of discipline and strength of will.

This sport metaphor used by Paul clearly shows how enduring hardship and bodily discipline can forge character. Certainly, there are different ways today to acquire self-control, but physical activity is particularly suitable for tempering a person's will in order to achieve self mastery.

The formation of the will can be compared to the strengthening of a muscle which occurs by exercising and stretching it. During training, muscle fiber is increased by undergoing strain. Stretching – placing tension on the muscles tendons – is also fundamental to strengthening the muscle's performance.

Something analogous occurs with our will. When one's will is put to the test and resists the "strain" to give up or give in, it is strengthened. Certain life situations can even test us or stretch the capacity of our will power to its utmost limits. In this way too, will power can be strengthened in these moments of greater intensity.

Moments of tension and strain abound in sport as well. An athlete constantly has to exercise his will power: before, during and after competition. In this way, sports activity implies much training that subjects the whole person to a strict discipline and subsequently a great deal of self-control is necessary. At times in physical training, the body feels exhausted and wants to rest, but the will pushes the person to persevere, to give more.

In the heat of competition as well, for example, when one is fouled at a crucial moment of the game, one has to exercise will power in order to keep one's passions in check. Then, there is a great temptation to loose one's composure. But a well formed will resist giving in to anger and disappointment …for he who allows passions and instincts to run wildly is similar to an animal, but he who reigns in his inclinations is a man.

Sport, therefore, is a tool that enables us to face life's trials. In this way too, discipline in sport it is an image and symbol of a "higher reality". Commenting on Paul's passage mentioned above, Pius XII noted:

> But what matters to the Apostle is the higher reality of which sport is an image and symbol: the unceasing work of Christ, the restraint and subjection of the body to the immortal soul, and to the eternal life which is the prize of this struggle. (May 20, 1945)

State of the art gyms will not suffice to elevate the human spirit. To overcome the hedonism and consumerism that entangles us, our society needs spirituality: virtues and values that transcend the material and a culture of "having". Because of this, the strain and discipline that go hand in hand with sport must also point to a higher reality. In this perspective, sport can assist the achievement of superior aims that are not necessarily linked to competitive results, despite their value. Sport is not man's end, but a useful tool to reach his end when used in an appropriate way.

Let us learn from St Paul the virtue of will power and self-control so as to ensure that after having practiced a hard discipline in sport, we don't get 'disqualified' for not having practiced the same disciplines in our daily duties and in our spiritual life.

Chapter 7

HANDLING VICTORY

Fight the good fight of the faith; take hold of the eternal life, to which you were called

1Tim 6: 12

When suffering a defeat it is important to remember that that it is only a game. The same applies to victory because success can easily inflate one's ego and make a person haughty. In today's hyper competitive society, it's necessary to teach young people about the danger of 'winning at all cost' and the importance of respecting the opponent. In this regard, Paul's teachings on the value and meaning of victory can be useful in forming a balance winning spirit.

Knowing how to win means knowing how "to manage" success in an appropriate way. There is nothing wrong in rejoicing in victory, especially after "having fought the good fight" in all fairness. But we must not forget that behind every success lurks the risk of an unhealthy pride that makes victor the end all and be all.

On the wall of the players' entrance to centre court at Wimbledon, are written these words: "If you can meet with Triumph and Disaster and treat those two impostors just the same!" This line from Rudyard Kipling's poem "If" helps all of us all realize that there is something illusory in victory as well a defeat. In this life, both are fleeting. Today's world record is broken next year. Next years championship is claimed by another…titles come and titles go. It is the person who remains.

At the end of a match, the scoreboard determines a winner and a loser. The winner has the right to be considered as such for to not do so would be false humility, for as St Teresa of Lisieux reminds us that "humility is the truth". Nevertheless, there is a deeper and more enduring truth that we also must keep in mind: we are not the author of our life and talents; they are gifts that come from God.

At times we see professional players acknowledging this truth when they lift their gaze and point upwards after scoring a goal as if to say that their success ultimately comes from their God given talent. Knowing how to win or to handle victory requires this proper perspective of humility. This will check our pride and not let the impostor of victory go to our head.

The value of rules

Knowing how to win also implies sportsmanship: honesty, integrity and fair play. In light of this, we recall that St Paul reminds Timothy that it's necessary to fight the good fight in an honest way, because no athlete receives his crown without playing by the rules (2 Tim 2:5).

Man cannot live in chaos, he seeks order and harmony. It is not possible to live without serious moral rules. It's not even possible to play a simple card game without rules. Against a culture of ambiguity, falsity, hypocrisy, calumny…we must answer with the pizzazz and fire of credibility. Clarity, transparency and responsibility are values that need to be lived and effectively promoted today more than ever before. Young people need rules and sports offer youth the transparency and clarity of precise rules. In fact, this is at the heart of what attracts spectators to sport as well as the player.

Every game has an established set of rules, times, spaces and absolute forms which gives it shape and a sense of order and beauty. Values cannot be transmitted from one generation to another by slogans. It is a task that must be fulfilled each day with our actions. We can't limit our Catholic presence to simply pointing fingers. It is necessary to lead by example. We need to show the youth a path to follow and offer them experiences to experience the beauty of ordered life that is derived from obeying rules.

Genuine victory will only be achieved by competing fairly. Any shortcut taken to reach a goal is only a deception where the player runs the risk of disqualification, or even worse, of damaging oneself altogether. Even though we must rely on God's help together with our own strength, there are no shortcuts in the Christian life! Therefore, if such fairness is demanded of athletes who work to get a corruptible crown, how much more must it be for the Christian who aspires for an eternal crown! (1 Cor 9: 25).

St Paul often uses the metaphor of the prize to talk about the victory of the faithful. In his letters we frequently find the expression "to crown the athlete" referring to he who has merited the prize. Yet he also uses the Greek word *brabein* (cf. 1 Cor 9: 24 and Phil 3: 14) which can also mean goal. Some biblical scholars think that Paul uses the image of the prize to show what can be achieved only through great effort and putting in all our energy. Others think that this word for prize refers to the goal line where the referee stands to determine the winner. Whatever the case may be, the Apostle is implying that all Christians are called to fight for the most important victory, where Christ himself, the just judge, will give us the crown of eternal life. For this reason, sport activities must be directed to this ultimate victory as well. In fact, in the bigger picture, as St Paul reminds Timothy: "physical exercise is of little use, while the exercise of piety is useful for everything, giving promise for life here and the life to come" (1 Tim 4:8).

Therefore, let us run to win in all fairness, always ensuring that our sports activity is a springboard and never a hurdle, to the attainment of our eternal crown.

CHAPTER 8

ACCEPTING DEFEAT

We are afflicted in every way, but not crushed; perplexed, but not driven to despair; persecuted, but not forsaken; struck down, but not destroyed...

2 Cor 4: 7- 9

To learn how to lose without feeling like a loser is a worthy goal for by every training program. At the end of a sports event the scoreboard shows the result and assigns a winner and a loser. When victory was ardently sought after but met only with a defeat it is only natural that ones enthusiasm wanes. But this is not the only "result" of the competition.

How can we learn how to accept defeat without despairing? Let's look at St Paul once again, taking as an example his first apostolic journey. If we compare the beginning of his first journey to the early weeks of a sports season, Paul certainly would have ranked in last place. Paul and Barnabas set off from Perga in Pamphylia to go to Antioch in Pisidia, covering 250 kilometers on foot – a journey of at least eight days. There Paul starts to proclaim the good news, but the local Jewish people expel him and Barnabas from the city.

After this first defeat, they then journey another 150 kilometers to Iconia. Here too he meets opposition from his own people, who spread ill will among the crowd to the point that they try to stone them. Paul and Barnabas escape for their lives to the town of Lystra and the score is now "0 and 2".Yet in Lystra, things get even worse: Paul is really stoned this time and believed to be dead! What a painful third defeat! But, he doesn't stay lying on the ground. With the help of the disciples, he gets up and starts his journey again in the direction of Derbe, persevering in his mission.

What would have happened to Christianity if Paul had stopped evangelizing? What would have happened had Paul not preached to the Corinthians, the Galatians, the Thessalonians or the Romans? All of us should learn from Paul this valuable lesson of not being overcome by immediate defeat; how to resist from without throwing in the towel in the face of difficulties.

In the second letter to the Corinthians, Paul frankly admits that loss hurts, but it is not despair: "We are afflicted in every way, but not crushed; perplexed, but not driven to despair; persecuted, but not forsaken; struck down, but not destroyed... (2 Cor 4: 8-9). Therefore, Paul doesn't get discouraged. On the contrary, defeat helps him acknowledge his own limits and renews his hope in Christ:

> Beloved, I do not consider that I have made it my own; but this one thing I do: forgetting what lies behind and straining forward to what lies ahead, I press on toward the goal for the prize of the heavenly call of God in Christ Jesus." (Phil. 3: 13-14)"

We often experience set-backs and failure in sport. These should be learning experiences that help to form the person. In fact, the real measure f Paul's success —and the same applies to us- is not the scoreboard, but in his ability to get back up on his feet. His secret to success is his attitude. St Paul does not remain lying on the ground, wallowing in his defeats. Instead, he gets back up and starts over again with even more determination.

Pope Paul VI, during an Audience with the cyclists of the *Giro d'Italia,* noted how sport is also a symbol of life as an ongoing effort towards a greater goal:

> Sport, more than just being a reality that is sensible and empirical, is also a symbol of a spiritual reality that is made up of the hidden, but essential goal of our lives. Life is an effort, a struggle, life is a risk, life is a race; life is a hope set upon a finish line which transcends the realm of common experience, where the soul intervenes and where religion presents itself. (May 30, 1964)

It is often said that an athlete is only a great champion when he can accept defeat and still play fair…But what do we do within this competitive culture in which only he who wins is valued, along with the one who is stronger and the one who produces more?

How many people seem incapable of accepting defeat! How many people seem bent on a 'win at all cost' mentality even to the point of fixing a match! For them, succeeding at life via defeat is not an option! Symptoms of these convictions are evident in the uneasiness of many young people who, when they find they can't achieve victory easily turn to escaping the reality of defeat (and life's limits in general) with drugs, alcohol, delinquency, even suicide! Yet, the question remains: why is it so horrible to lose? Why is it so difficult to accept defeat?

It is difficult to accept defeat in a world that pushes you to be a winner, to get the top results at any cost; in a word where who and what you are is dictated by outward results –

by what you wear or what you achieve- and not on what is deep within you. Young people especially fear the idea of being excluded from the race, of not to being associated with "the cool ones". Yet, even though it can cause tears and an emotional crisis, the sooner they learn this valuable lesson of accepting defeat and their own limits the better it will be for them.

We know all this is easily said, but difficult to live…but, life offers us ample occasion to practice this! On the other hand, losing is not always a bad thing. Defeat in sport means that, today, somebody else has won and, tomorrow, maybe it will be our turn.

Learning to accept defeat will help us to become a better person because the defeat gives us new energy, a lot of strength to improve our performance and become true winners. Life is one match after another: sometimes we win, sometimes we lose, but we always need to compete again.

This is the secret of success in life, knowing how to start over again, never getting discouraged, never abandoning the race, never losing sight of the finish line. Courage, sacrifice, patience and enthusiasm are necessary, but above all it requires mental strength. Our Lord Jesus Christ gave us the example of the grain of wheat that must die in the furrow in order to bear fruit. As long as the grain doesn't die to itself and put out new shoots, it will never become a new blade of wheat. To know how to lose helps us to grow and to mature in order to bear fruit; the key is to set out all over again with ever more enthusiasm.

CHAPTER 9

TEAMWORK

Live your life in a manner worthy of the gospel of Christ ...
standing firm in one spirit, striving side by side with one mind
for the faith of the gospel...

Phil 1: 27-28

A team player must respect the fundamental role of each of his team mates while being able to sacrifice his own glory or personal gain for the benefit of the team. Because of this, teamwork is one of the noblest dimensions of sport as it calls for a unity that transcends differences of personal salaries or individual talent. In fact, often we see professional teams with great financial resources and star players losing to teams equipped with a smaller budget, fewer stars, but a stronger spirit of collaboration and team work.

Certainly the players that put themselves on the line to make an assist for their team mates don't appear in the sports headlines but they make an indispensable contribution to the effective performance of the team.

As we are immersed in a culture dominated by individualism and selfishness, we feel the need more than ever to rediscover the value of teamwork because this virtue is just as essential for team sports as it is for the fundamental peace and harmony of family, professional and community life.

St Paul, despite his strong character and firm will, proved himself to be a team player. Ever since that very first encounter with Christ on the road to Damascus, he quickly understood the "team play" that was implied in belonging to a body of believers, all members of the one "mystical body of Christ". Even though he had strong leadership qualities, he knew how to respect each person's role and, whenever necessary, he could put others before himself. For example, we can see how Paul, before starting his first apostolic journey, accepted having to wait 'on the bench', as he remained patiently in Tarsus until 'selected' by Barnabas for a mission. Only then Paul starts to proclaim the word of God.

Another aspect of team play in Paul was his ability to respect the proper fields of apostolate that were already being evangelized. As a team player, Paul decides to go where no other apostle had yet gone before – respecting the work of the others and never losing sight of Peter as the chosen leader. Paul's ability to become "all things to all men" and sacrifice himself for the good of the mystical body is epitomized in his initiative to take up a collection for the poor in Jerusalem, regardless of risking his own life in order to see that this offering reached its final destination.

Additionally, like all good coaches, Paul knew how to promote teamwork among his flock. In relation to this, we read in the letter to the Philippians: "stand firm in one spirit" and "strive side by side with one mind for the faith of the Gospel" (Phil 1, 27-28). When there was a controversy in Corinth among the believers, with some factions saying: "I belong to Paul", and others: "I belong to Apollo", the apostle admonished them with these words "I urge you, brothers, in the name of our Lord Jesus Christ, … that there be no divisions among you, but that you be united in the same mind and in the same purpose" (1 Cor 1: 10-12).

In several papal speeches we also find references to the extraordinary ability of sport to form this essential virtue of team work. Blessed John Paul II, in his words to the soccer players of AC Milan, illustrates the spiritual dimension of team work:

> A team is not only the fruit of physical qualities and strength; it is also the result of a wide range of human virtues, from which its success depends such as: understanding, collaboration, friendliness and communication. In a word, these are all spiritual values, without which a team cannot exist and has no effectiveness (May 12, 1979).

The late and great college basketball coach John Wooden defines team work as the eagerness to lose oneself in the group for the good of the group. Wooden backs this up with the specific case of UCLA's 1964 basketball team. He noted that this team had an unusual *espirit de corp* because it had no one superstar. Any one of the five might have been a top scorer in a game. But even more importantly, it did matter who would be the top scorer because they knew that if the five of them operated as individuals non of them would be effective.

Therefore, let us "stand firm in one spirit" against this culture of selfishness, and "strive side by side" with one mind and one heart as the very first Christians, generously sacrificing our egoism for good of the team and for the good of the entire Mystical Body which is the Church.

CHAPTER 10

PERSEVERANCE

*Beloved, I do not consider that I have already reached the goal;
but this one thing I do: forgetting what lies behind and straining
forward to what lies ahead... I press on to make it my own.*
cf. Phil 3: 12-14

We live in a world dominated by a "disposable" mentality; a world so obsessed with pleasure, that relentlessly seeks for a short cut rather than the arduous road of sacrifice. We take a pain killer for the slightest headache; we constantly flip the television channel to escape boredom or the fatigue of intellectual stimulation.

In this context it is certainly not easy to learn perseverance, which is the virtue that enables one to stay focused in the pursuit of a goal without changing direction or giving up as soon as it becomes tiring. The opposite habit of getting distracted easily and not be able to complete a work in progress, has serious and delayed consequences in life. When work becomes difficult, we can't simply change job. The same applies to marriage or relationships: when it's hard we can't just dismiss our commitments for the illusion of a 'freer' life without these responsibilities.

In order to rectify this mentality or deficiency, we need to exercise the virtue of perseverance. The dictionary describes it as "a constant steadfastness of attitude, motivated and sustained by firmness of purpose".

Perseverance doesn't mean stopping in front of a difficulty or attempting to escape from it, but rather implies going 'through' it! In fact, it comes from the two Latin words *per* (through) and *severus* (difficulty), which means 'getting through difficulty'. Therefore, perseverance doesn't depend upon external circumstances, but is purely rooted in the will. It is the ability to keep focused on the target, the aim, the goal.

In the 110 meter hurdles event in athletics, the hurdles are an essential part of the race. Nobody would consider removing them as they are there to be overcome. In the face of obstacles, it is necessary to have more strength, determination and fighting spirit. Goals cannot be reached by only making a decision; one must also act, by getting involved, following through, even if this implies risking failure.

In sport, perseverance is also a mental quality that enables an athlete to overcome an injury or another setback that might test one's patience. The apostle Paul -in the first person singular- describes this attitude very well in his letter to the Philippians:

> Not that I have already obtained this or have already reached the goal; but I press on to make it my own, because Christ Jesus has made me his own. Beloved, I do not consider that I have made it my own; but this one thing I do: forgetting what lies behind and straining forward to what lies ahead, I press on toward the goal for the prize of the heavenly call of God in Christ Jesus (Phil 3: 12-14).

A first point to be noted here is St Paul's sense of focus. Like a runner, it is fundamental to never lose sight of the goal or the prize that awaits us. Before reaching the finishing line, we should above all desire to get there.

Secondly, once the person is focused on the goal, there is a second moment that comes into play in the action of perseverance. Paul expresses it with the verbs *diokein* and *katalambaneim* that mean "to speed up" and "to grasp" the goal. From these verses, it seems that Paul is almost obsessed with attaining his goal, so bent is his drive and determination to reach it. St John Chrysostom, referring to this passage in Paul, observes that the runner is not thinking about how many times he has already gone around the track but only about how far he has still to go.

Afterwards, Paul uses another very descriptive verb: *epekeinesthai*, which means "to lunge forward" or "to rush" to the finish. In fact, athletes, during a sprint, push their body forward in order to be faster. In other words, mediocrity or the status quo won't cut it. Perseverance requires giving that something extra that lies deep inside. We, as St Paul , need to make this kind of extra effort.

How can sports help to form young people in the virtue of perseverance? One way is by the demands of time that each game places on the players. Just as in a race, a runner cannot stop until he reaches a finish line, a game is not over until the last second of the clock has ticked, until the whistle blows. The match must be played till the last minute and, on some occasions, those last minutes are particularly important if the team is losing or winning.

A champion athlete always gives her best – not only when the team is winning, but also when it is losing. At stake here is not only victory, but also the formation of this virtue. In fact, even when defeat is imminent, playing one's best until the very end is a sure way to forge this virtue.

There is another aspect of perseverance to consider. Young people tend to quickly lose the initial enthusiasm that they had at the outset. This especially can apply to sport. By sticking to what they have committed themselves to, young people learn perseverance. We need to encourage them to finish the season right down to the last match, regardless of results, or whether their initial enthusiasm disappears, or whether they are sitting on the bench.

It is important for them to remember that they made a commitment at the beginning of the season to the other players to be a part of the team regardless of the results. So if a young person wants to remain true to his commitment to the team, he needs to persevere, giving his best to the very end of the season. In doing so, what a valuable lesson we can help them learn now that will come in handy tomorrow in persevering in their commitments, whether it be to a spouse, to raising a family, or to other lofty tasks.

CHAPTER 11

CHAMPIONS IN LIFE

Do you not know that in a race the runners all compete,
but only one receives the prize?
Run in such a way that you may win it.

1 Cor 9:24

What does it really mean to be a champion? What is St Paul getting at when he encourages the Church at Corinth to "run in such a way as to end"? He further qualifies this statement saying that he himself does not run aimlessly nor does he want to be disqualified (cf. 1Cor 9:26, 27). Paul is obviously not talking about a track meet, but rather, an underlying attitude that gives purpose to our lives and impels us to press on "toward the goal for the prize of the heavenly call of God in Christ Jesus" (Phil 3:14). It is a winning attitude and the true spirit of a champion. In fact, the difference between a champion and a mediocre person is the level of enthusiasm, courage, patience, endurance, determination, passion and commitment -for this is what pushes a champion to strive after a goal, to give their best, to train, to compete, to be a team player, to be a winner.

Some have claimed that what counts in sport is simply to take part. Taking part is essential but a champion thirsts for more. A champion seeks excellence, and a part of excellence is striving to win, honestly and without cheating. Life is a race, a great match in which we can win, lose or draw. Anyone can be a champion as long as they are ready to live courageously and with clear objectives to be achieved. Young people who learn how to compete are more capable of overcoming the hurdles and obstacles of life. Whoever succeeds in confronting life without giving up, will have certainly lived purposefully, because even defeat becomes a stimulus to do better in future. On the other hand, whoever expects victory without hard work is living in a dream and such a mentality can even lead to dishonesty.

What else does it take to be a champion? A champion is also aware of his or her own resources and abilities, as well as their personal limitations. While respecting these limits, they pursue clear goals while putting into action their entire being.

Competition gives life flavor

We know very well that competitiveness is an energy of extraordinary value. Facing life with a competitive spirit leads us to develop our will power, our endurance and our ability to sacrifice for the sake of clear and achievable goals. There is no doubt that competition causes the level of technique and performance to be raised. At the same time, we must be aware that unbridled competition can also be lethal if it does not respect the needs and limits of the person with a healthy dose of realism to boot.

As we have seen, the development of personal aptitudes, whether sport related or those employed for other human endeavors, is achieved through the strengthening of competences and technical training. Improving competences requires gaining specific knowledge related to them as well as developing certain behavioral skills. Technical training demands ongoing discipline that perfects mental exercise and physical performance.

Nonetheless, many youth – who are either adolescents cooped up in padded after school day care facilities, or young adults trapped in a holding pattern for years while awaiting a job an occupation, don't often have the opportunity to develop skills and competencies and consequently are not able to grasp these demands and urgencies placed upon them by life. Thus when challenges arise of when they are misunderstood, they become confused and anxious because they don't have the correct motivation or the skills to respond appropriately.

It is alarming that many teens don't play much sport because they don't make the team. Many coaches think that only a select group of talented and physically gifted individuals can really become champions. Yet this is not the case, as will power, motivation, enthusiasm, discipline and perseverance are necessary too. Precisely because of this, it is worth the effort to create opportunities –such as those afforded by sport– that assist young people to become aware of their inadequacies and sensitive to them in order to eventually overcome them.

Having the right motives

Therefore, in light of the great potential that can come from investing in youth sports we need to first set out the proper motives that should determine how sport's activities are to be organized and carried out. The overarching motive is that of offering a sport that is at the service of life and the realization of a person's fullest potential. Only in this way will sport provide a horizon within which values, and this mentality of a champion- can be implemented.

The longing for success, self confidence, and a sense of belonging are some of the most fundamental dynamics that underpin of the human being and his actions. Consequently, any activity that seeks to respond to these human "needs" with patience, determination and humility can sustain and direct the human person in a positive way. These deep motivations push a person to test himself and face new challenges, yet they are nourished and met especially when they are supported by the family, social groups or other social structures that are full of values, spirituality, and genuine human concern. This is due to the fact that all of these motivations need to be placed within the context of a shared human experience and also require real guides who can inspire and motivate others to imitate the values that they live.

We can easily see how having the right motivations is the foundation of success in sports. Especially when these motivations enable one to enjoy the personal satisfaction that comes from an individual reaching their utmost best with regards to their psychological and spiritual conditions.

This attitude is also a necessary condition for endurance and for achieving one's goals in sports. The right motivation –which starts from within oneself -is the background for playing sport with pleasure. Therefore we must offer young people the right motivations for engaging in sport and not just any strange whim or fancy. The act of choosing infers that there are some programs 'more suitable' than others for each individual, in keeping with the person's inclinations and complex identity.

Let's suggest some specific motivations that should characterize and identify young people's commitment to sport, and encourage an involvement capable of interpret the complex personalities of young people. These motivations are closely related to the three needs previously mentioned needs: the need for success, for a sense of belonging and for self confidence. The goal of all of this is to develop a strategic plan for offering the youth those motivations that are already rooted in these deeper motivations that tend to sway their actions and behavior both positively and negatively.

Ascetic motivation

Asceticism is a must for anyone who wants to successfully reach their goals. If young people really want to have success -in the sense of happiness and fullness that satisfies both the body and the spirit- they must learn to fight, to have a spirit of discipline that is characterized by temperance – as St Paul claims: "The athlete is temperate in everything" (1 Cor 9:25). Commenting on this passage of St Paul, John Paul II noted the following:

> The logic of sport is also the logic of life: without sacrifices, important results are not obtained, or even genuine satisfaction. (…) Every Christian is called to become a strong athlete of Christ, that is, a faithful and courageous witness to his Gospel. But to succeed in this, he must persevere in prayer, be trained in virtue and follow the divine Master in everything. He, in fact, is God's true athlete: Christ is the "more powerful" Man, who for our sake confronted and defeated the "opponent", Satan… [Christ] teaches us that, to enter into glory, we must undergo suffering… (October 29, 2000).

Yes, our goals can only be achieved through effort and daily commitment. Consequently, it's necessary for us to convince and educate young people about commitment and sacrifice. And we should be bold in doing so, for this goes directly against today's current where tendencies of ethical indifference, wide spread laxity, and a general lack of zest for life are carrying many downstream.

Asceticism implies undergoing a type of "agony" in the Greek sense of a personal struggle; it is the personal stance taken by one who wants to prevail from a state of discomfort, uneasiness or difficulty. It is the resolution taken by the individual to ready himself in order to face his opponent or some other adversity. It is the attitude of Our Lord Jesus Christ, who, at the end of his night long agony in the garden of Gethsemane, goes forth to face his betrayer and the guards, boldly responding: "I am he!" (Jn 18:5).

For all of these reasons, the ascetical motivation is an integral part of a "course for champions" and it is the necessary and opportune response to the eventual -and even at times unavoidable- defeats of life. In other words, we need to transmit the spirit of a champion that enables one to keep their poise, remaining calm and in control in adversity. To do so, we ourselves, need to posses this genuine enthusiasm that enables us to be leaders who are capable transmitting this spirit to others.

Group motivation

Those who work with youth and parents know how much young people need to be accepted and need to feel part of a group. As beings who are in constant emotional evolution, continually experiencing dramatic mood shifts and contrasting frames of mind, they tend to be stabilized by a this sense of group belonging.

Here we touch on the something very sensitive – the emotional aspect that attracts and engages young people. Here there is a great need for truth and authenticity. At the same time, in this regards, adults must learn to be able to lead them discretely, with wisdom and example, aware that there is always a right time and a right place, and a right ways to do so. There are moments when silence is more appropriate than words, and other moments when the "right words" are needed to break the silence.

Young people need to learn how to handle their emotions and feelings and they need to learn how to handle and establish important relationships. Therefore, it is not a matter of flattery but of truly helping them to improve themselves. All this needs to take place in an environment of truth and mutual respect, free from any hidden agendas. They can come to simply experience that they are valued and loved through the kindness and genuine attention shown towards them.

In this way, sports activities can be harmoniously inserted into the context of the emotional development of young people, alongside personal talks, career guidance, and other social, cultural and religious initiatives. The key is that all of this takes place and can take place precisely because there is a climate of sincere care and fruitful dedication on the part of the educator.

Group association has always been a dynamic and decisive element that enables the individual to feel part of something greater than himself, and gives one an identity and making them part of a history. Association can happen naturally, as in the case of a family, or can be created by election, as in the case of sport. Sport represents an powerful opportunity for association: a specific time and place for gathering for a purpose. Sometimes this is merely occasional or spontaneous gathering, but in every case it is an opportunity for socializing. It's being together for a purpose and this stands in contrast to the boredom of loneliness and the emptiness of life. In order to combat this aspect of youth culture we must invest in resources strategically aimed to improve the quality and sense of the free time experiences.

Overcoming the disarray of young people's free time implies an understanding the reasons behind their lack of interests and removing habitual resistances which are often the fruit of a poor formation, or intentional or unintentional marginalization. Such negative conditioning can lead young people to extreme situations involving forms of social transgressions and misdemeanors. On the other hand, when group association is directed in the right way, it fulfills its original purpose of creating a strong sense of sharing and the real exchange of ideas. It strengthens common bonds through the involvement in shared experiences. All of which can be achieved in sport in a unique way.

Competitive motivation

Striving for excellence- this competitive spirit- is for courageous people and not for the timid or mediocre. It is the stuff of champions: for those who want to win and not lose. Yet, it is an action in favor of life, and not of death. It is more about being, than about having. As we know competitiveness is strongly related to sports activity. Consequently, success and personal achievement cannot be excluded from it, especially in the educational context. It's just a matter of giving a boost to those quiet youthful energies and by developing a plan that will have an effect on young people's sensitivity and ability to react.

In competitive confrontation young people become aware of their capabilities, of their real potential and ability 'to get their head in the game' with a clear and conscious strategy. Sport has rules and demands that must be respected and maintained with determination and conviction. 'Emulation' is part of healthy competition, part of overcoming apathy's obligations, part of getting rid of common prejudices. It presumes that the person knows himself, his body, his capabilities, his ability to react, to endure and confront. In other words it is a matter of never forgetting the internal drive for self-betterment, to win, to take pride in giving one's best. It requires an understanding that what counts are the values related to "confronting" oneself with another and not the confrontation itself.

Today especially, young people are thirsting for a new source of inspiration. They are in need of true guides – effective leaders whose character is deeply rooted in authenticity– who can convey self-confidence. For this reason the winning mentality of a champion is what is most needed, and this has to be sustained and supported by a network, fortified by fundamental and solid principles and animated by a spirituality that is at the service of the human person.

As we have seen throughout this book, properly guided sports activities can foster a quest for excellence, a healthy competitive spirit, and prompt the deeper motivations mentioned above which are all indispensable ingredients in order to succeed in life and reach the ultimate goal.

St Paul set a course for champions by confronting the hardships and setbacks of an Apostle with heroism and perseverance. His life was ultimately crowned, not with a perishable wreath, but with the eternal wreath of martyrdom! Two thousand years have passed since but the legacy of this champion of the faith lives on. The "agon motif" so present throughout his letters continues to speak to the champion within each one of us and spurs us on.

In light of all of this, it only fit to conclude this course for champions with the same words with which St Paul described his own life as he was about to approach the earthly finish line and enter into eternity:

> I have fought the good fight, I have finished the race, I have kept the faith. From now on there is reserved for me the crown of righteousness, which the Lord, the righteous judge, will give me on that day (2 Tim. 4: 7-8).

APPENDIX

THE SPORT VIRTUES IN THE POPES

Many of the popes in the last century have highlighted sport's capacity to serve as a means for the development of qualities and virtues compatible with the Christian life. While not being afraid of pointing out sport's limits and while warning us of its possible deviations, the pontiffs have acknowledged its formative capacity and have also elevated this human activity by including it within the horizon of the faith. So, as a further supplement to this course on the sport virtues found in the writings of St Paul, we offer you a sampling of some of the specific words pronounced by some of the recent popes regarding the relationship between sport and the human virtues we have considered throughout this book.

Pope Pius X (1903-1914)

St Pius X met with Baron Pierre de Coubertin in 1905 and presided over several gymnastic displays that were held in the Vatican courtyards of Belvedere and St Damase. To the youth participating in an International gymnastic and sport contest that was held in Rome in 1908, St Pius X had these affectionate words:

> To you, dear young people, I speak from the heart. After such a fine demonstration, I congratulate you not only for your talent, but also for the expression of your faith which animates you. I praise, admire,

esteem, and bless all of your gymnastic games, exercises, races, alpinism, and other similar activities. May all of these pursuits that you do reach the end for which they were intended. Indeed, I praise and bless these activities because they provide exercise for your body and elevate your spirit; also because they enable you to flee from idleness which is the root of all vices and they enable you to exercise virtue in these fraternal competitions.

Pope Pius XI (1922-1939)

Years before Pius XI became pope, he was experienced alpinist who had climbed to the top of Mt Rosa. In an audience with Alpine guides who were gathered in Rome for their national convention, Pius XI offered this list of virtues that he himself found among the Alpine guides that helped him and with whom he even shared in great challenges:

> ...a sense of focus, steadfast spirit, courage, calmness, prudence, and even at times ambition, a just ambition that is derived from the certainty of being able to overcome difficulties. To this list can also be added a noble sense of one's duties and responsibilities. (November 16, 1929).

In his Encyclical *On Christian Education*, Pius XI stated:

> It must never be forgotten that the subject of Christian education is man whole and entire, soul united to body in unity of nature, with all his faculties natural and supernatural...." (n. 58).

Subsequently, Pius XI noted in the same Encyclical the contribution that youth sports can make in an overall Christian formation of the person:

> This educational environment of the Church ... also includes the great number and variety of schools, associations and institutions of all kinds, established for the training of youth in Christian piety, together with literature and the sciences, not omitting recreation and physical culture. And in this inexhaustible fecundity of educational works, how marvelous, how incomparable is the Church's maternal providence! (n. 76)

Pope Pius XII (1939-1958)

Pius XII made the following commentary regarding St Paul to the newly born Catholic *Italian Sports Center* association:

> And let no one reprove St. Paul his bold expression: "I buffet my own body and make it my slave" (1 Cor. 9:27). For in that same passage, Paul is basing himself on the example of the keen athletes! You are well aware from personal experience that sport, undertaken with conscious moderation, fortifies the body, gives it health, makes it fresh and strong, but to achieve this work of education, it subjects the body to a rigorous discipline which dominates it and really makes it a slave: training in stamina, resistance to pain, a severe habit of continence and temperance, are all indispensable conditions to carry off the victory.

Sport is an effective antidote to softness and easy living. It awakens the sense of order, and forms the man in self-examination and mastery of self, in despising danger, without either boasting or cowardice. So you sec already how it goes far beyond mere physical strength, and leads man to moral strength and greatness. This is what Cicero with incomparable lucidity of style expressed when he wrote: "Exercendum... corpus et ita afficiendum est, ut obeodire consilio rationique possit in exsequendis negotiis et in labore tolerando." "The body should be so treated and trained as to be able to obey the counsel of wisdom and reason, whether it be a matter of work to be done or trials to be borne."

From the birthplace of sport carne also the proverbial phrase 'fair play': that knightly and courteous emulation which raises the spirit above meanness and deceit and the dark subterfuges of vanity and vindictiveness, and preserves it from the excesses of a closed and intransigent nationalism. Sport is the school of loyalty, of courage, of fortitude, of resolution and universal brotherhood: all natural virtues, these, but which form for the supernatural virtues a sound foundation, and prepare man to carry without weakness the weight of the greatest responsibilities. (May 20, 1945)

In a meeting with the directors of the Central Sports School, a military sports programs on the campus of several American universities, Pius XII had these encouraging words:

Sport, properly directed, develops character, makes a man courageous, a generous loser, and a gracious victor; it refines the senses, gives us intellectual penetration, steels the will to endurance. It is not merely a physical development then. Sport, rightly understood, is an occupation of the whole man, and while perfecting the body as an instrument of the mind, it also makes the mind itself a more refined instrument for the search and communication of truth and helps man to achieve that end to which all others must be subservient, the service and praise of his Creator. (July 29, 1945)

On the tenth anniversary of the foundation of the *Italian Sports Center*, Pius XII again return to the theme of the virtues of the athlete:

Educating through sport seeks among other things to form the youth in the virtues that are proper to this activity. These are, among others: loyalty that does not permit the use of subterfuges, docility and obedience to the rules that guide the exercise of teamwork, a spirit of self denial that when tempted to fraudulently seek your team's advantage; fidelity to one's commitment, modesty in victory, generosity towards the defeated, serenity before one's victors and adverse fortune, patience towards the immoderation of spectators, justice if highly competitive sport is linked to financial interests freely contracted, and in general, chastity and temperance which were already recommend in antiquity. All of these virtues, even if they have as their immediate object physical activity which is exterior, are genuine Christian virtues, that cannot be acquired and exercised in their highest degrees without an deep religious spirit and, we also add, without frequent recourse to prayer. When practiced in this way, and inserted into the supernatural horizon, sport can be almost a type of *ascesis*, for the Apostle St Paul urged us to refer to God every action that a Christian does (1Cor. 10,31). (October 9, 1955).

Pope John XXIII (1958-1963)

During a papal audience with members of a professional soccer team from Spain, Pius XII exalted the educational value of sport:

> Sport and especially the game of soccer, can be a school of virtue; of individual virtues in our own perfecting that often requiring much self-sacrifice in order to persevere in difficult moments, much commitment to giving what is right to give in every circumstance, much strength of spirit to know how to lose without getting upset, much love to know how to win without humiliating the opponent; of social virtues, especially in accepting the role given in the team, in the tactics that have to be applied at that moment, they sacrifice personal initiative, enabling the dynamic of the team to operate fully within the complexity demanded by modern tactics, without selfishness, vanity or personal issues, with that particular discipline that makes the athlete a good example for those who sincerely desire to adopt Christian self-denial in every area of their life (July 6, 1956).

Pope John XXIII underlined the bond between sport and virtue in his words of address to the *Italian Sports Center* National Congress:

> Sport has in our life an immense value for the exercise of virtues... Even in sport, in fact, true Christian virtues can be developed and then be established and made fruitful by the grace of God. : in the spirit of discipline one learns and practices obedience, humility, self denial; in team play and competition, charity, fraternity, reciprocal respect, magnanimity, and sometimes even pardon; in the strict demands of physical performance, chastity, modesty, temperance and prudence (April 26, 1959).

On the very Feast of the Conversion of St Paul, at the first Italian Catholic national sports congress, John XXIII made this eloquent commentary with regards to two of St Paul's sport metaphors:

> It seems most fitting to have chosen as the date for today's encounter January 25th, Feast of the Conversion of St Paul... Observe how the celebration of this liturgical day with the wonderful pages taken from the Acts of the Apostles – and narrate the interior and exterior discipline with which molded the life and apostolate of the Apostle *ad gentes*– underlines well the Church's interest in all ages for the reaching at this perfect equilibrium between soul and body. The figure of Paul the Apostle -with his enterprising spirit and body tempered by extreme physical endurance- is particularly attractive to young people, who are by nature generous, ardent, enthusiastic and prone to imitation. Additionally, in his Epistles, St Paul demonstrates an ample

knowledge of the sporting life of his time and adapted it into vivid examples that illustrate the highest moral truths. The prize offered to contestants in the race, offers a metaphor for the effort with which one must run on the path of virtue and sacrifice: *sic currite ut conrprehendatis* (1Cor. 9: 24); the exemplary sobriety of the athletes to achieve a human-made crown inspires a generous invitation to temperance and vigilance to obtain a crown of eternal happiness. (1 Cor. 9,25); the skills of a boxer who does not wish to strike at the air speak of firmness and precision, which must be practiced as well in the Christian struggle: "I do not run aimlessly, nor do I box as though beating the air; but I punish my body and enslave it, lest after preaching to others, … I myself should not be disqualified" (1Cor. 9: 26). And at the end of his life from his cell in Rome, with his body held captive, but the diffusive action of his apostolic spirit shinning more brightly than ever, he could write to the disciple Timothy: "I have fought the good fight, I have finished the race, I have kept the faith. Henceforth, a crown of righteousness awaits me" (2 Tim. 4: 7-8). These valuable indications can enlighten and guide your actions that seek to form ones character and will through the educational effectiveness of physical effort, which is loyalty, security, self-mastery. This is all the more true if you are convinced that these magnificent results cannot be fully achieved without making use of one's spiritual qualities also. We spoke of this in the fore mentioned Olympic audience: "the rules of a healthy family education and youth formation demand that you be on guard so that it is not exclusively the body that is sought after as the highest good of the person, and that the passion for sport does not hinder the integral fulfillment of one's duties. You should always appreciate and encourage fairness in physical exercises and nobility in the competitions of the gym. Indeed, there are many valuable and numerous talents that can be developed through sport; regarding the body: health, strength, coordination, grace; regarding the soul: endurance, strength, and the practice of self- denial. (January 25, 1963)

Pope Paul VI (1963-1978)

Regarding the virtue of will power and self control, Pope Paul VI offers us these helpful observations:

> Jesus preaches self-denial, renunciation that his disciples themselves must undergo. St Gregory tells us that this implies not only the renunciation of external things but also the giving up of one's inner self (Hom. 32 in Ev.: PL 76, 1232) when it wants to refuse to give God the honor that is due to him in order to peruse its own selfishness and idolatry. The hardest type of self-denial is this: that which fights against self-exaltation. But, if we recall the Beatitudes, it is also the most blessed. This is the essence of penance, this is the gospel.
>
> Here we must insist upon two observations in order not to be misunderstood. The first is that we must be motivated to discover how this teaching —which is severe for our own ego- does not distract us from recognizing the value and goodness of the external world, nor does it dispense us from the obligations

we have towards it during our life on earth (cf. *Gaudium et Spes*, 4).

The second observation reminds us that Christian self-denial, mortification, and penance are not forms of weakness, nor an "inferiority complex", but rather, they are manifestations of personal fortitude and results that stem from the efforts of grace and will. These qualities help us to appreciate the transcendent value of our actions; these train us in self-mastery, they give unity and balance to our faculties, enabling the spirit to prevail over the flesh, reason over fancy, will over instinct; they induce into our being a need for completeness and perfection, which we can even sometimes call holiness. Where there is rigor there is also vigor. (March 7, 1973)

Inspired by the old adage *mens sana in corpore sano*, Paul VI highlighted the cardinal virtues in his Message to the Olympic Games of Montreal:

Together with you, we think of self-control over our own body. What a need for perseverance and tenacity! Doesn't inner strength find an important place among the four cardinal virtues? Doesn't the ascesis of sports people, mentioned by St Paul in his first letter to the Corinthians, remind us of the virtue of temperance? Isn't their key responsibility to train themselves and prepare for competition close to prudence? Isn't acknowledging the ability of all players, the impartial refereeing, the fair play of those defeated, the controlled triumph of the winners, a call to practice the virtue of justice? And if all these moral virtues contribute to the fulfillment of the human being, how can they have no repercussions on society? (July 16, 1976).

Pope Paul VI stresses how a well-run sports program can and must be for the youth a school of various virtues:

> By developing and refining a person's physical and psychological potential, sporting activities contribute to a more complete human maturity. As you well know, it is for this reason that the Church looks with sympathy to those who dedicate themselves with intelligence and foresight to the promotion of sport. You also know the urgency with which we ourselves, on repeated occasions, have called directors and athletes of different sports to dutifully seek in these physical exercises not only to reinforce the body's strength, prowess and agility, but also the harmonious development of that spiritual energy which is necessary for a just orientation of the instincts and passions and without which would be otherwise detrimental to the balanced unfolding of personal and social life. We would like to reiterate on this occasion our sincere appreciation for the unique opportunities that a well-run sports training includes in itself: the youth can and must find in it a very effective school of loyalty, self-control, courage, dedication, fraternal cooperation... In short, it is a school of those values that, while uniquely human, are the indispensable foundation of spiritual values which Christianity praises and endorses. (March 23, 1978)

Pope John Paul II (1978-2005)

Pope John Paul II pronounced these words in the light of St Paul and sport in an audience with presidents of the Italian sports federations, gathered in Rome for the meeting:

> The Church has always been interested in the problem of sport, because she prizes everything that contributes constructively to the harmonious and complete development of man, body and soul. She encourages, therefore, what aims at educating, developing and strengthening the human body, in order that it may offer a better service for the attainment of personal maturation. The body, according to Christian concept, deserves due interest, real respect, loving and wise care, invested as it is with natural dignity, capable of a mysterious sacrality and destined to ultimate victory over death itself, as our faith teaches us. I like to repeat with St. Paul: "Glorify God in your body" (cf. 1 Cor 6:20).
>
> Certainly, the value of the body must be supported and pursued in respect of the hierarchy of the higher moral and spiritual values, which, sometimes, require sacrifice of physical life itself, in order to affirm the absolute primacy of the spirit, of the soul, created in the likeness of God, reborn to new life by the sacrifice of Jesus Christ, the Incarnate Word, and called to the imperishable wreath, alter the happy accomplishment of the earthly competition (cf. 1 Cor 9:24-25). Practiced in this outlook, sport has in itself an important moral and educative significance: it is a training ground of virtue, a school of inner balance and outer control, an introduction to more true and lasting conquests. (December 20th, 1979).

With the occasion of the World Athletics Championship being held in Rome, Pope John Paul II had these thoughts to share on the virtues of sport:

> We all know that sport is a highly disciplined exercise of the human body. It seeks to develop a person's physical faculties, such as strength, stamina, skill —all working together towards a harmony of movement and action. Through sport we try to attain physical excellence, by means of necessary training and practice. Its aim is perfection in a given event, as well as the breaking of significant records, as has already happened during these competitions.

> However, there is another dimension to sports activity. Sport is also an important moment for guaranteeing the balance and total well-being of the person. In an age that has witnessed the ever-increasing development of various forms of automation, especially in the workplace, reducing the use of physical activity, many people feel the need to find appropriate forms of physical exercise that will help to restore a healthy balance of mind and body.

> And from here arises that special interest and attention to sporting events, which today attract great masses to athletic competitions of every kind. This phenomenon exposes you athletes to considerable psychological pressures because people tend to extol you as heroes, as human models who in spire ideals of life and action, especially among youth. And this fact places you at the center of a particular social and ethical problem. You are observed by many people and expected to be outstanding figures not only during athletic competitions but also when you are off the sport field. You are asked to be examples of

human virtue, apart from your accomplishments of physical strength and endurance. (September 2, 1987)

We can recall three lessons that John Paul II drew from Paul's letter to the Corinthians, in his homily during the International Jubilee of Sport, held in Rome's Olympic Stadium in 1984:

> In the first place, sport is making good use of the body, in an attempt to reach optimum physical condition, which brings marked consequences for psychological well-being. From our Christian faith we know that, through baptism, the human person, in his or her fullness and integrity of soul and body, becomes a temple of the Holy Spirit: "Do you not realize that your body is the temple of the Holy Spirit, who is in you and whom you have receive from God? You are not your own property, then; you have been bought at a price (that is, with the blood of Christ the Redeemer). So use your body for the glory of God" (1Cor 6,19-20).
>
> Sport is competitiveness, a contest to win a crown, a trophy, a title, a first place. But from the Christian faith, we know that the "imperishable crown," the "eternal life" which is received from God as a gift but which is also the goal of a daily victory in the practice of virtue is much more valuable. And if there is a really important form of striving, again according to St Paul it is this: "But earnestly desire the higher gifts" (1 Cor 12,31), which means the gifts that best serve the growth of the Kingdom of God in yourselves and in the world!
>
> Sport is the joy of life, a game, a celebration, and as such it must be properly used and perhaps, today,

freed from excess technical perfection and professionalism, through a recovery of its free nature, its ability to strengthen bonds of friendship, to foster dialogue and openness to others, as an expression of the richness of being, much more valuable and prized than having, and hence far above the harsh laws of production and consumption and all other purely utilitarian and hedonistic considerations in life (April 12, 1984).

Pope Benedict XVI

Pope Benedict XVI also brings out the relationship between the virtues and sport when addressing professional skiers:

> Many look up to you, not only for your noteworthy sporting achievements, but also for the virtues and values that are characteristic of your sport: perseverance, determination, spirit of sacrifice, internal and external discipline, attention to others, team work, solidarity, justice, courtesy, and the recognition of one's own limits, amongst others. These same virtues also come into play in a significant way in daily life and need to be continually exercised and practiced.
>
> In fact, you, dear athletes, shoulder the not insignificant responsibility of bearing witness to these attitudes and convictions and of incarnating them beyond your sporting activity into the fabric of family life, culture, and religion. In doing so, you will be of great help to others, especially the youth, who are immersed in a rapidly developing society where

there is a widespread loss of values and growing disorientation (October 6, 2007).

While at his summer residence in Castel Gandolfo in August of 2009, Pope Benedict gave an audience to athletes participating in the national swimming championships that were being held in Rome. Here are some of the words from his speech to them in which he comments on how sport can be a precious instrument for the perfection and balance of the whole person:

> ...sports, practiced with enthusiasm and an acute ethical sense, especially for youth become a training ground of healthy competition and physical improvement, a school of formation in the human and spiritual values, a privileged means for personal growth and contact with society. Watching these swimming championships and admiring the results achieved make it easy to understand the great potential with which God has endowed the human body and the interesting objectives of perfection it is able to achieve. One then thinks of the Psalmist's wonder who in contemplating the universe, praises the glory of God and the greatness of man: "when I behold your heavens", we read in Psalm 8, "the work of your fingers, the moon and the stars that you have set in place what is man that you are mindful of him, or the son of man that you care for him?" (vv. 3-4). Then, how can one fail to thank the Lord for having endowed the human body with such perfection; for having enriched it with a beauty and harmony that can be expressed in so many ways?
>
> The sports disciplines, each in a different way, help us to appreciate this gift which God has made to us.

The Church follows and encourages sport, practised not as an end in itself, but as a means, as a precious instrument for the perfection and balance of the whole person. In the Bible we also find interesting references to sport as an image of life. For example, the Apostle Paul, considered sports an authentic human value and used them not only as a metaphor to illustrate lofty ethical and ascent ideals but also as a means for human formation and as an element of human culture and civilization." (August 1, 2009)

Since its establishment by John Paul II in 2004, the "Church and Sport" section of the Pontifical Council for the Laity has held periodic seminars regarding various aspects of pastoral care of the vast world of sport. With occasion of its third International sport seminar entitled: "Sport Education, Faith: Towards a New Season for Catholic Sports Associations", Pope Benedict XVI made the following observation in his Message to Cardinal Stanislaw Rylko, President of the Pontifical Council for the Laity:

> Through sports, the ecclesial community contributes to the formation of youth, providing a suitable environment for their human and spiritual growth. In fact, when sports initiatives aim at the integral development of the person and are managed by qualified and competent personnel, they provide a useful opportunity for priests, religious and lay people to become true and proper educators and teachers of life for the young. In our time when an urgent need to educate the new generations is evident it is therefore necessary for the Church to continue to support sports for youth, making the most of their positive aspects also at competitive

levels such as their capacity for stimulating competitiveness, courage and tenacity in pursuing goals. However, it is necessary to avoid every trend that perverts the nature of sports by recourse to practices that can even damage the body, such as doping. As part of a coordinated, formative effort, Catholic directors, staff and workers must consider themselves expert guides for youth, helping each of them to develop their athletic potential without obscuring those human qualities and Christian virtues that make for a fully mature person. (November 3, 2009)

ABOUT THE AUTHORS

EDIO COSTANTINI

Edio Costantini is from San Benedetto del Tronto (Italy). From his many years of involvement with Catholic Action, he has seen how sport can serve as an important educational tool for young people. In 1991, he left the business world to fully dedicated himself to the service of Catholic youth in Italy as national secretary of the *Italian Sports Center* (CSI) and later as its president from 2000 to 2008. Currently he is the director of the CSI's national think tank as well as president of the John Paul II Sports Foundation and adviser to the Pontifical Council for the Laity.

KEVIN LIXEY, LC

Father Kevin Lixey, a native of Flint, Michigan, was ordained a priest of the Congregation of the Legionaries of Christ in 2001. In 2004 he was appointed by John Paul II to begin the 'Church & Sport' section within the Pontifical Council for the Laity (www.laici.va) who entrusted it with the following goals: 1) to insure a more direct and systematic attention to the vast world of sport on the part of the Holy See; 2) to solicit a renewed sensitivity on the part of the local Church in this field; 3) to promote a culture of sport in harmony with the true dignity of the human person; 4) to conduct studies and investigation concerning particular problems and challenges regarding sport; 5) to promote initiatives that can serve to evangelize the world of sport.

THE JOHN PAUL II SPORTS FOUNDATION

The John Paul II Sports Foundation aims to promote the educational values of sport. It follows the principles and guidelines of John Paul II and the pastoral teaching of 'Sport & Christian Life' of the Ecclesiastical Commission for the Pastoral of Leisure and Sport of the Italian Episcopal Conference, with special care towards the world's youth. It seeks to be at the service of the initiatives of the 'Church and Sport' Section of the Vatican's Pontifical Council for the Laity and the National Office for the Pastoral of Leisure, Tourism & Sport of the Italian Episcopal Conference.

www.johnpaul2sportfoundation.org

To purchased a copy of this book, visit:
www.lulu.com/sport&stpaul

Made in the USA
Middletown, DE
16 January 2020

83303260R00066